MIND RENEWAL TRANSFORMATION DEVOTIONAL Vol. 3

Presented to

_____

By

_____

Date

_____

MIND RENEWAL TRANSFORMATION DEVOTIONAL Vol. 3

A 30-Day Transformational Journey

LEOSTONE MORRISON

Charlestown, Nevis W.I.

Copyright © 2020 by Leostone Morrison
PRINT ISBN-13: 978-1-62676-567-2
ALL RIGHTS RESERVED

Without limiting the rights under copyright reserved above, no part of this publication may be reproduced, stored in or introduced into a retrieval system, or transmitted, in any form, or by any means (electronic, mechanical, photocopying, recording, or otherwise), without the prior contractual or written permission of the copyright owner of this work.

. . . . .

Published by
Restoration of the Breach Publishing
Lou-Mot Drive Colquhoun Estate,
Charlestown, Nevis W.I.
restorativeauthor@gmail.com
Tele: (869) 669-4386

Ebook Cover Design by Tevaun Brown
tbartgraphic@gmail.com

Formatting and Publishing done by Sherene Morrison

Unless otherwise stated Scripture verses are quoted from the New King James Version of the Bible

Author Contact
For consultation, feedback or speaking engagements contact the author at restorativeauthor@gmail.com

PRAISE FOR THE MIND RENEWAL DEVOTIONAL SERIES

I reviewed the Mind Renewal Devotional Vol2. I must say, this is a powerful devotional book. It spoke into my life from the very first chapter. I was one to live in shame, fear, and guilt. It took me a long time to forgive myself for the all the things I went through and allowed in my life. I built up a stronghold in my mind and pretended that everything was okay when this was far from the truth.

This devotional took me on a journey of self-discovery and mind renewal. Throughout the journey, the assignments helped to weed out negative mind-sets and keep me accountable to progressing along the path of spiritual maturity. I learnt that "all things work together for good to them who love God, to them that are called according to his purpose." (Romans 8:28). All things include all the pain that I have been through and the scars that remain.

This devotional has also inspired me to be a witness of the gospel, in hopes that the lost will come into the saving knowledge of the Lord Jesus Christ, and those who are saved will continue to have their minds renewed.

Thank you Rev for availing yourself to the Lord for Him to use you in this manner.

I was richly blessed!

Anika McNaught

Educational Assistant-Child and Youth Care

This book is dedicated to Next Level Let's Climb WhatsApp Bible Study Family. Daily we meet and share from the word of God. You have been a source of inspiration and encouragement for me. I thank the Holy Spirit for daily inspiration as various teachings are presented. We have all grown together.

Love you my family.

INTRODUCTION

Who will stand against the dictated established order of the mind of the world? That which the world system has engraved in your mind will not be overruled simply because it is a new desire. This will require intentional pursuit of change. Although change is vitally necessary, it is usually resisted. However, that resistance to mental transformation must be counteracted with matching or improved resistance. The Word of God supports this proposal according to James 4:7, which reads, "Therefore, submit to God. Resist the devil, and he will flee from you." (NKJV). For resistance against the mind of the world to be effective, you must first submit to the Mind of God. Philippians 2:5 exhorts us with the following words, "Let this mind be in you, which was also in Christ Jesus." (NKJV). Jesus was aggressively tempted by the mind of the world, but the Mind of Christ resisted and secured victory. Like for Jesus, victory on all dimensions of your existence is available and should be pursued relentlessly.

This is volume 3 of the three-part devotional series, Mind Renewal Transformation Devotional. You, through the help of the Holy Spirit, have navigated through volumes one and two and have reaped the wealth thus far. Let your harvesting continue as you excavate the fruit of this final volume. If this is your first volume, volumes 1 and 2 awaits you.

This 30-Day Mind Renewal Transformational Devotional serves as a guide to your continued transformation. This volume has five parts which covers topics dealing with your next, trusting God, denied, perspectives and vision vs sight.

Use it alongside the Mind Renewal book. This devotional is equipped with transforming stories, supporting, scriptures, assignments, and a daily journal page. The journal page is to be used to document your daily assignments, challenges, and victories. The advice of the previous volumes continues; do not move on to another day before completing the assignment and journal of the present one. Please continue to expand and demonstrate your new mind culture.

The Better You is at hand.

TABLE OF CONTENTS

Introduction   VII

PART 1: NEXT

Day 1-Don't Let Bitterness Take Your Glory---------------1
Day 2-Heavy Dreams and Visions---------------------------4
Day 3-Shut Mouth, Concealed Mind-------------------------7

PART II: TRUSTING GOD

Day 4-Greater Odds, Greater Victory---------------------11
Day 5-Lenses of God-------------------------------------14
Day 6-Guaranteed Completion-----------------------------18
Day 7-Locked Minds Don't Fight--------------------------21
Day 8-Make the Step-------------------------------------24
Day 9-Your Best Days Are Ahead Of You-------------------27

PART III: NO LONGER DENIED

Day 10-God of Crisis and Solution-----------------------30
Day 11-Shift--34
Day 12-Shift into Victories-----------------------------37
Day 13-Physical Bars vs. Spiritual Freedom--------------40
Day 14-Sanctuary unto God-------------------------------43
Day 15-Freed To Impact----------------------------------46

Day 16-Where Is Your Treasure? ---------------------------49
Day 17-Transferred Wealth---------------------------------52

PART IV-SEE THINGS DIFFERENTLY

Day 18-Defiled By Your Words-----------------------------56
Day 19-Change History------------------------------------59
Day 20-Challenged Dogmas---------------------------------62
Day 21-There Is No Glory in the Usual--------------------65
Day 22-Benefit of Past Victories-------------------------68
Day 23-Amplified Testimonies-----------------------------71
Day 24-Seeing Beyond Closed Doors------------------------74

PART V: VISION INSTEAD OF SIGHT

Day 25-Perspectives--------------------------------------79
Day 26-Visions vs. Sight---------------------------------82
Day 27-Become a Planner----------------------------------85
Day 28-In Spite Of!--------------------------------------88
Day 29-Vision Supersedes Sight---------------------------91
Day 30-Unique By Your Flaws------------------------------94
BONUS: Day 31-Cracks and Flaws---------------------------97
CONCLUSION--100
ACKNOWLEDGMENTS---102
ABOUT THE AUTHOR--104

PART 1: NEXT

NEXT

Day 1.
Don't let bitterness take your glory

Scripture Focus: Ruth 1

Quite often we are presented with the option of bitterness or glory. We might not be able to boast that we have always chosen the path that leads to glory… In the book of Ruth, Naomi said the following:

"Now the two of them went until they came to Bethlehem. And it happened, when they had come to Bethlehem that all the city was excited because of them; and the women said, "Is this Naomi?" But she said to them, "Do not call me Naomi; call me Mara, for the Almighty has dealt very bitterly with me. I went out full, and the LORD has brought me home again empty. Why do you call me

MIND RENEWAL TRANSFORMATION DEVOTIONAL

Naomi, since the LORD has testified against me, and the Almighty has afflicted me?" Ruth 1: 19-21 (NKJV)

The name Naomi means pleasantness and Mara means bitter. Basically, Naomi said, "My glory has departed from me. God has stripped me and clothed me with bitterness." The fullness she spoke about was her husband and two sons. Unfortunately, all three died.

Jesus was also presented with the option of bitterness or glory. In Luke 22:48, Jesus addressed Judas with the words, "but Jesus asked him, "Judas, are you betraying the Son of Man with a kiss?" Jesus referred to him despite his evil act, as a friend. You must not allow a person's evil doings to convert you into becoming bitter.

Renew your mind with this truth: You can choose between bitterness and glory. Choose glory. Jesus did not demonstrate any negative feelings toward Judas. Instead, he maintained his classification of him. He had chosen him to be part of his ministry… Despite his evil act, Jesus never cursed or banished him. He secured his glory.

What has made you bitter, and for how long now have you surrendered your glory? Was it the loss of a child, a marriage, an abortion or being treated as the outcast of the family? Is it a failed business venture, being wrongfully dismissed from your job or an opportunity stolen by a friend or family member? Whatever it is, it is time to retake your glory. Leave no more room for bitterness!

NEXT

ASSIGNMENT

1. Deep soul search and identify and list the cause of all bitterness.
2. Purge yourself of the bitterness.

Document your responses to the assignment as well as your challenges and victories.

MIND RENEWAL TRANSFORMATION DEVOTIONAL

Day 2.

Heavy dreams and visions

Scripture Focus: Genesis 37: 5-11

Dreams and visions are wealth to be realized. They can serve as instruments of futuristic planning. The success of your future is not to be approached with triviality. According to Proverbs 29:18a, "Where there is no vision, the people perish." I have been the recipient of dreams and visions that were outside of the realm of immediate reach; dreams so far beyond my present situation, I dare not to speak.

Eric S Young wrote:

I have started two companies. When starting the first, I told lots of people and asked for their advice - I was so fearful at the time. Almost all gave me negative feedback. Finally, I stopped asking and just started the firm. The more

NEXT

I followed my intuition, the more success I had. As the company grew, the more fear I succumb to and the more I returned to asking and following other people's advice. I made too many mistakes near the end and the company failed. The second firm I started has been successful and I am not telling anyone about it.

Eric had his vision of operating a company. He shared his dreams and was flooded with negatives. After failing once, he adopted a different approach – just do it. The wrong person getting a hold of your dreams can function as the key in locking your dreams in dream land. The negative feedback can be stemming from the weight of the dream you shared. The weight is crushing, and the negative feedbacks are suffocating.

In Genesis 37, Joseph had dreams of his brothers and parents bowing to him. This caused him to be hated by his brothers and rebuked by his father. He was only seventeen, yet they could not handle the weight of his dreams. They were not equipped to bear the burden of this futuristic truth. Renew your mind with this truth: you may do an injustice to persons by sharing your dreams and visions because not everyone is equipped to handle their wealth and weight.

ASSIGNMENT

1. Carefully evaluate who you share your dreams with.

MIND RENEWAL TRANSFORMATION DEVOTIONAL

2. Don't allow negative feedback to paralyze you from pursuing your dreams.

Document your responses to the assignment as well as your challenges and victories.

_____
_____
_____
_____
_____
_____
_____
_____
_____
_____
_____
_____
_____
_____
_____
_____
_____
_____
_____
_____
_____

Day 3
Shut mouth, concealed mind

Scripture Focus: Mathew 12: 34b

As a child growing up, I remember seeing a plaque on the wall with the inscription: "Lord help me to keep my big mouth shut." My understanding minimized the message as I arrogantly thought about a literal big mouth. However, the depth of the message lies in this - an open mouth exposes your mind.

Jesus expressed this truth in Matthew 12:34b which states, "For out of the abundance of the heart the mouth speaks." (NKJV). Whatever the state of your heart/mind is, the mouth will make it known. James 3:8 declares "But no man can tame the tongue. It is an unruly evil, full of deadly poison." (NKJV) This Scripture points not just to the tongue, but the fountain from which it flows –the mind. If

MIND RENEWAL TRANSFORMATION DEVOTIONAL

the tongue is distributing deadly poison, it means the mind is poisonous.

Some years ago, two friends met and were talking. Girl A said, "I met a nice guy, please help me pray. I need to know if he is God's will for me." Girl B agreed to pray. Girl B kept her promise and prayed. The response she got was, "no, not the will of God." She tried to get in contact with her friend, but to no avail. Sometime later, they met.

Girl A was already married and parading a beautiful ring, but she was not happy. She said, "One day, they had an argument and he stormed out of the house... Then returned and said in a very unusual voice and tone, "I have come to destroy your life". Then he walked away. She never knew he was on an assignment until he spoke. His words exposed his mind. His mind was poisonous towards her and laced with destruction. He pretended well until his mouth exposed the true him. If we listen more, we will know more. Mouths are revealing, but are we listening?

ASSIGNMENT

1. Please pay more attention to the expressed words of people.

Document your responses to the assignment as well as your challenges and victories.

NEXT

MIND RENEWAL TRANSFORMATION DEVOTIONAL

PART 2: TRUSTING GOD

Day 4.
Greater odds, Greater victory

Scripture Focus: Exodus 3 and 14

William Tyndale was convinced that everyone in England—from the Palace to the subjects should have access to the Bible. He acted on his convictions and challenged the position of the church and King, which were both reluctant to provide English language copies of the Bible to the mass.

The odds against Tyndale were great. The price was massive as it cost him his life. But the victory won was priceless. In the company of death, he prayed that the Lord would defend His cause. His victory did not just help make the Bible accessible to households in England, but to many others around the world.

MIND RENEWAL TRANSFORMATION DEVOTIONAL

Like Tyndale, the odds were stocked against Moses. He knew the odds were against him. He expressed this as he spoke with God in Exodus 3:10-11 where God told him to go to Egypt and deliver the children of Israel from slavery.

Moses had to return to Egypt where he had killed a man and ran away. Pharaoh had an army with weapons but all he had was the word of God. In Chapter 14:28, we see all the Egyptians who pursued the children of Israel drowned as the once parted water returned to its place. Moses went in obedience to God against the odds and witnessed a magnificent victory over Pharaoh.

ASSIGNMENT

1. The next assignment where the odds are against you, don't panic. Pursue.

Document your responses to the assignment as well as your challenges and victories.

_____
_____
_____
_____
_____
_____

TRUSTING GOD

MIND RENEWAL TRANSFORMATION DEVOTIONAL

Day 5

Lenses of God

Scripture Focus: 1 Peter 2: 1-19

In her blog, impaired vision…. Alicja Oshiokpekhai wrote the following:

When I was younger I would look in the mirror and see only "imperfections." My gap, lack of curves, my "nappy" natural hair. I began to weigh my worth based on my physical features, and unfortunately, that wasn't the only worldly thing that I tied my worth to. I also found value in what others had to say about me. I was "too sweet, too sensitive, annoying, too loud, too quiet, and not adventurous enough." Not only did that lead me to a vast amount of insecurities, but it also drove me to constantly change myself to match whatever beauty trend was popular at the time; it lead me to try and accommodate everyone's opinion of who and how I should be. I looked for my worth in just about anything but God.

If you are going to be successful, you must be adamant to see yourself from the lenses of God. What does God see when He looks at you? According to Zechariah 2:8, "For thus says the LORD of hosts: "He sent me after glory, to the nations which plunder you; for he who touches you touches the apple of His eye." (NKJV). You must renew your mind to the place of embracing the love of God for you. The sins that you committed are no longer before God. He sees you through the righteousness of Jesus. Micah 7:19 puts it this way, "He will again have compassion on us, and will subdue our iniquities. You will cast all our sins into the depths of the sea." (NKJV).

The exhortation continues, according to 1 Peter 2:9, " But you are a chosen generation, a royal priesthood, a holy nation, His own special people, that you may proclaim the praises of Him who called you out of darkness into His marvelous light;" (NKJV). You are seen not from the sins of your past, nor from the perception of your peers, but as one who is special to God and called to show His glory on the earth.

ASSIGNMENT

1. Research in depth and adopt to your consciousness how God sees you.

MIND RENEWAL TRANSFORMATION DEVOTIONAL

Document your responses to the assignment as well as your challenges and victories.

TRUSTING GOD

MIND RENEWAL TRANSFORMATION DEVOTIONAL

Day 6.
Guaranteed Completion

Scripture Focus: Mark 8: 22-25

Many projects or assignments get birthed but die shortly after. As you travel the world, you will see unfinished buildings, ranging from houses to plazas. A good example is the famous church of Barcelona, a major tourist attraction, which is still under construction after 130 years. The beauty is the determination to bring it to completion.

We know God is greater than man. God is not one who starts what He is not able to complete. When He began creation, He never rested until He competed his creation... In Mark 8: 22-25 we see Jesus completing the restoration work of brining a man from darkness into light:

Then He came to Bethsaida; and they brought a blind man to Him, and begged Him to touch him. So He took

TRUSTING GOD

the blind man by the hand and led him out of the town. And when He had spit on his eyes and put His hands on him, He asked him if he saw anything. And he looked up and said, "I see men like trees, walking." Then He put His hands on his eyes again and made him look up. And he was restored and saw everyone clearly. (NKJV)

God has begun a good work in you, which is the renewing of your mind. You must therefore partner with God on this journey. Reject the pull to return to where you departed.

ASSIGNMENT

1. What did you give up on God completing?
2. Make a list and get back to the assignment.
3. Don't lose hope. God will complete it.

Document your responses to the assignment as well as your challenges and victories.

_____

_____

_____

_____

_____

_____

MIND RENEWAL TRANSFORMATION DEVOTIONAL

Day 7
Locked minds don't fight

Scripture Focus: Mathew 19:16-23

Harry Houdini was a master magician and locksmith. He boasted about being able to escape from any prison cell. Avani Mehta wrote the following about Houdini:

"A small town in the British Isles built a new jail cell and they were proud of it. "Come give us a try," they said to Houdini, and he agreed. He walked into the prison cell bristling with confidence. After all, he had done this hundreds of times before. Houdini hid inside his belt a special lock pick he had designed. Once the jail cell was closed, Houdini took off his coat, and set to work with his lock pick. But he discovered that something was unusual about this particular lock. For 30 minutes he worked and got nowhere. And his confident expression disappeared. An hour passed, and still he had not been able to open the door.

MIND RENEWAL TRANSFORMATION DEVOTIONAL

By now he was bathed in sweat and panting in exasperation, but he still could not pick the lock. He tried all the tricks of his trade, but nothing worked. After two hours and totally exhausted, Houdini literally collapsed against the door. The door swung open and he discovered it had not been locked in the first place! It was locked only to him in his mind.

Houdini tried desperately to open that which was not locked physically. He was using physical tools to open a mental lock. His mind was locked into a deception. Like Houdini, there are doors that are opened unto you but have the look and stench of being closed. Let not the locks of your mind ruin the possibilities of your present and future.

In Mathew 19, we are introduced to a rich young ruler. He kept the law, but Jesus told him to sell his possessions, give to the poor and come follow him. But he walked away sorrowful because he had many possessions. The young man's mind was locked to his earthly wealth which restricted him from seeing the heavenly treasures that awaited him. If the enemy succeeds in locking your mind, he will never have to fight you again. A locked mind cannot receive from the fountain of abundance.

ASSIGNMENT

1. With all you have within you, keep your mind open and prepared to receive from God.

TRUSTING GOD

Document your responses to the assignment as well as your challenges and victories.

MIND RENEWAL TRANSFORMATION DEVOTIONAL

Day 8
MAKE THE STEP

Scripture Focus: Joshua 1: 1-18

It might seem like thousands of stairs before you but if you were able to see and count them, it would be easy. The reality is, you will only see step three after you have walked step two. The uncertainty of how each stair will unfold is nerve-wrecking. The constant voices of living safely, fear and doubt are daunting, and make us apprehensive about taking the next step. Truth is, you will never know what you would have missed out on, until you make the step.

17-year-old Meryl from Lima, Peru writes, "Before applying to the National University of San Marcos, I was very nervous and I thought I couldn't do it, but one week before the admission exam I got a beautiful letter from my sponsor. She sent me this verse in Joshua 1:9 to be strong and brave, don't be afraid; do not be discouraged, for the Lord my God will be with me wherever I go. And I entered the university in the first try, and now I am studying biology!" said Meryl. She is the first in her family to go to college. Now in her second year of studies at university, she's also a volunteer at her Compassion-assisted child development center and a private math tutor.

Meryl made the step, one that she had no reference from family to emulate. As you pursue the renewal of your mind, please understand, you are called to think and act unlike the examples of peers and family. Meryl received a timely encouragement from her sponsor, one that Joshua the newly appointed ruler of the children of Israel received from God.

God encouraged Joshua three times, and the people once, to be brave and courageous. Joshua's assignment was, "arise, go over this Jordan, you and all this people, to the land which I am giving to them—the children of Israel." God further told him, "Every place that the sole of your foot will tread upon I have given you, as I said to Moses." (Joshua 1:2-3). (NKJV). Victory awaited him and grasping it began with taking the first step. Your victory is near.

ASSIGNMENT

1. No more excuses. Take the step!

MIND RENEWAL TRANSFORMATION DEVOTIONAL

Document your responses to the assignment as well as your challenges and victories.

Day 9
YOUR BEST DAYS ARE AHEAD OF YOU

Scripture Focus: Jeremiah 29:11

Before incarceration, a spiritual daughter of mine, lived the fast lane. She did parties, money, alcohol, and drugs. She got sentenced to five years behind walls at which time she was pregnant. She did not know her best days would begin in prison. A Christian group led by Pastor Karel Dawes visited and had a service. My daughter accepted the Lord Jesus Christ as her personal Savior. She began reading and studying the word of God. She was released and attended services with Pastor Dawes. Many doors have been closed to her because of her prison history but many have also been opened to her.

MIND RENEWAL TRANSFORMATION DEVOTIONAL

She had the awesome opportunity of being invited by the prison authorities to do ministry at the facility. She got saved there and went back to minister the Gospel of Jesus. Inmates with whom she served, saw her as representing hope. Maybe, their best days are yet to be lived.

I heard Bishop T.D. Jakes say in a message, "You have not sung your best song, laughed your best laugh nor lived your best day yet." What if your best days are yet to be lived? The decision to renew your mind catapult you into your best days. Your best days are yet to be lived. No longer shall you be a victim to the errors of your past nor the dictates of society. A renewed mind cannot be imprisoned. Your freedom days have begun… No more chains!

ASSIGNMENT

1. List five ways you can pursue your best life as you continue to renew your mind then aggressively pursue!

Document your responses to the assignment as well as your challenges and victories.

_____
_____
_____
_____
_____
_____

TRUSTING GOD

MIND RENEWAL TRANSFORMATION DEVOTIONAL

Day 10

God of crisis and solution

Scripture Focus: 1 Samuel 30: 1-8

The late Reggae Super Star, Bob Marley said, "Every man thinks his burden is the heaviest." This is true, until you try to lift the burden of another. King David experienced burdens of magnanimous dimensions. One such is recorded in 1 Samuel 30. Now David was greatly distressed, for the people spoke of stoning him, because the soul of all the people was grieved, every man for his sons and his daughters. David and the soldiers went to war and upon their return, their wives and children were all taken captive and the city burned.

I personally have received many breakthroughs upon the acceptance of this mind renewal truth: God knows your crisis and He knows the solution. Upon their return home, David and the soldiers were met with empty homes. This took them by surprise! But not God. The almighty God is all knowing. This present crisis that has you baffled and crying did not throw God into a panic.

I love what David did: he strengthened himself in the LORD his God. In our time of crisis, let's follow David's example. He inquired of the Lord. "Then David said to Abiathar the priest, Ahimelech's son, "Please bring the ephod here to me." And Abiathar brought the ephod to David. So David inquired of the LORD, saying, "Shall I pursue this troop? Shall I overtake them?" And He answered him, "Pursue, for you shall surely overtake them and without fail recover all." 1 Samuel 30:7-8 (NKJV)

God gave David the solution to the crisis...the crisis that almost had him stoned. Rather than becoming depressed, frustrated, or getting to the place of cursing God, please be reminded that it is not a crisis to God. In Jeremiah 32:27 the Lord says "Behold, I am the LORD, the God of all flesh. Is there anything too hard for Me? (NKJV). God knows the answer, therefore, run to Him.

ASSIGNMENT
1. The crisis that have you perplexed, inquire of God what is the solution.
2. Pursue His instructions.

MIND RENEWAL TRANSFORMATION DEVOTIONAL

Document your responses to the assignment as well as your challenges and victories.

PART 3:
NO LONGER DENIED

Day 11
SHIFT

Scripture Focus: Galatians 5:13-26

In Genesis Chapter 1, we see God in the spiritual realm orchestrated and created the physical domain. It stands to reason that the spiritual realm existed before the physical domain. Humans are spiritual and physical. Unfortunately, we give more attention to the physical than the spiritual. Daily you wash, groom, clothe, perfume, and rest your bodies, but how much time do you allocate for the soul and spirit?

Galatians 5: 16-17 says the spirit and the flesh (body) are contrary to each other; they are at war and will always remain fighting. The one we give more attention to will be the one that directs us. Verse 25 of the same chapter says, "If we live in the spirit let us also walk in the spirit." (NKJV). A young man was staying at a friend's home because he was experiencing trying times. His bathing soap was finished but he didn't want to be a bother, so he used the powdered soap. One morning two friends came to see him, bearing gifts of bar soaps. One said, the Lord told her, his soap was finished, and he was in need of soap. She received instructions from the Holy Spirit, and she acted on it. The Spirit realm knows what the physical realm is oblivious to.

Hear this perspective! You have been confined to the physical realm when the spiritual realm awaits you with embracing arms. To receive the victories you long for will require you to shift your focus and place the spirit realm above the physical. You must pay more attention to your soul and spirit.

ASSIGNMENT
1. Stop ignoring the Holy Spirit as He speaks to you. It might not be logical or intellectually rational, however, be obedient.
2. Refuse to be only guided by the flesh. Shift focus to the spirit.

Document your responses to the assignment as well as your challenges and victories.

_____
_____
_____
_____

MIND RENEWAL TRANSFORMATION DEVOTIONAL

Day 12
Shift into victories

Scripture Focus: Ephesians 6:10-18

A husband was dissatisfied in his marriage and wanted to be released from it. He went into prayer, seeking God's permission to leave. As he prayed, the Holy Spirit told him to pray for his wife. He redirected his prayer as instructed. He realized, whenever he prayed, there was peace between them, but when he ceased, there was animosity. He enquired, "God, will I always have to be fighting?"

The first recorded fight was not in the physical realm but the spiritual. This was the fight between spirits. Lucifer and his converted angels lost the battle and were expelled from the Kingdom of God. God then created the physical realm and in Job 1:7, God asked Satan (Lucifer) where he was coming from, and he responded, "From going to and fro on the earth." (NKJV)

The two existing domains are the spiritual and the physical. Battles are fought in both realms. We see in the book of Daniel in chapter 10, a battle being fought between angelic beings. Daniel received a vision and wanted understanding of the same. He went into fasting and did so for twenty-one days. The angel of the Lord was sent to give him understanding.

The angel of God was hindered by the Prince of Persia, a spirit of the kingdom of Satan. Another angel, Michael from the Kingdom of God, was sent to assist the hindered one. The spirit realm (Heaven) gave the physical realm (Daniel) a vision and this caused a fight in the spirit realm. The spirit realm decided to favour Daniel with the answer, but his opposition was also directed from the same realm. Ephesians 6 tells us we wrestle not against flesh and blood (humans) but against spirits. Your physical celebration depends on your spiritual victory!

ASSIGNMENT
1. Stop fighting your battles from the physical plains.
2. Research and implement how to fight in the spiritual domain.

Document your responses to the assignment as well as your challenges and victories.

NO LONGER DENIED

MIND RENEWAL TRANSFORMATION DEVOTIONAL

Day 13
Physical bars vs. Spiritual freedom

Scripture Focus: Acts 16:23-26

My wife shared a video with me of a circus elephant, a massive animal, tied to a small shrub by a piece of rope. The rope and shrub were miniscule in comparison to the strength of the elephant, yet it had him bound. The narrative suggests that the elephant was trained to believe that he was bound once the rope was tied to its foot. He was cultured and believed that the rope and shrub decided on its boundaries.

Similarly, there are persons who are imprisoned without knowing that they are bound. The greater imprisonment is that of the mind and the spirit, where one is physically free, but spiritually bound. Until a man's mind is free, he may be loose externally but bound internally.

NO LONGER DENIED

In Acts chapter 16, Paul and Silas, despite being physically abused through flogging and incarceration, their expressions of spiritual freedom stood as a testimony to the other prisoners. All were imprisoned but not all were bound. Just because we share the same space does not mean we are identical in our consciousness. They were singing unto God after just being beaten and imprisoned for God!

Let it resonate in our spirits that an attack against your belief should serve to strengthen it and not cause a departure from it. Whom Jesus has set free, is free indeed. Are you free? Has fear paralyzed you in any way? Now, it's time to paralyze fear. Doubt your doubts and live the free life.

ASSIGNMENT
1. What is it that has limited you, preventing you from living the free life Jesus gave unto you?
2. Take charge of your life. You will not defeat what you have not confronted.
3. Make a list of things to confront and pursue.

Document your responses to the assignment as well as your challenges and victories.

_____

_____

_____

_____

MIND RENEWAL TRANSFORMATION DEVOTIONAL

Day 14
SANCTUARY UNTO GOD

Scripture Focus: 2 Chronicles 6: 17-40

Weekly, we get dressed and attend our favourite sanctuaries to worship, pray and give honour to God. This is a good practice. According to Hebrew 10:25a "Not forsaking the assembling of ourselves together." (KNJV). These sanctuaries are made of materials like stones, blocks, boards, and steels. 2 Chronicles 6:40 speaks to Solomon's dedication of the temple he had built unto the Lord. In his dedication as he prayed about the altar, he said, "Now, my God, may your eyes be open and your ears attentive to the prayers offered in this place."

According to 1 Corinthians 6:19, your body is the temple of God. I listened to the old refrain, penned by Randy Scruggs and John Thompson, "Lord prepare me to be a sanctuary." I realized their message echoes this truth. It shifts the focus from the man-made sanctuary to you and me, who were created by God. If the man-made sanctuary has an altar, it stands to reason that the temple of God, you and I have altars or are altars. What takes place at our altars?

Solomon said, "Whoever comes to this altar, hear and heal them." Now as the sanctuaries of God, we speak from the altars of God. Therefore, whomever we pray for or whose lives we speak into Lord let it be done. This we pray in faith standing on the words of Jesus Christ in Mathew 21:22, "And whatever things you ask in prayer, believing, you will receive." (NKJV)

ASSIGNMENT
1. Let yesterday be the last day you do not see yourself as a sanctuary unto God.
2. You are an altar unto God. Change your perspective.
3. Everything you do or say is done from your altar. Ensure your sacrifices are holy and pleasing to God.

Document your responses to the assignment as well as your challenges and victories.

_____
_____
_____
_____
_____
_____

NO LONGER DENIED

MIND RENEWAL TRANSFORMATION DEVOTIONAL

Day 15

Freed to impact

Scripture Focus: Luke 23:24

A former neighbour of mine, recounted her grandmother's final last moments alive. She was at the hospital with her family around the bed. But rather than having a sad moment, they watched her as she worshipped and rejoiced in God. Her physical body had come to the place of separation, but her spirit was moving onto unification with Jesus. She departed in peace.

Apostle Joshua Selman said, "A dying man does not ask for more possessions, he asks for time." This is true but when Jesus was on the cross, He asked His father to forgive those who were crucifying him. He was contented in death. He was dying in the physical but free and alive in the spirit.

Relatedly, like my former neighbor and her family were impacted by her grandmother on her dying bed, the people who heard Jesus' prayer on the cross were impacted. His spiritual freedom impacted the physical realm. Jesus modelled a renewed mind: forgiving in the midst of his pain. As you demonstrate your spiritual freedom, persons who come in contact with you, will be challenged and positioned for change. The positive impact will foster well needed transformation.

ASSIGNMENT
1. Make a list of all those who have hurt you, whom you have not forgiven.
2. Forgive them wholeheartedly as God forgave you.
3. Make up your mind to quickly forgive those who hurt you.

Document your responses to the assignment as well as your challenges and victories.

_____
_____
_____
_____
_____
_____
_____
_____
_____

MIND RENEWAL TRANSFORMATION DEVOTIONAL

Day 16

Where is your treasure?

Scripture Focus: Colossians 3:1-4

We grew up watching movies and cartoons about pirates hiding or going in search of hidden treasures. Some of the terrains they journeyed were rough and life threatening. But they were not daunted by the possibilities of injury or death. They kept their focus on the potential prize that awaited them, safely hidden from the average eyes. They had no guarantee that they would find treasures. Yet they were determined to explore upon the premise of maybe.

We are not as unfortunate as the pirates, who searched on maybes. We are guaranteed mansions in heaven. We are exhorted from Colossians 3: 1-2 "If then you were raised with Christ, seek those things which are above, where Christ is, sitting at the right hand of God. Set your mind on things above, not on things on the earth." (NKJV)

We are called to function from a higher dimension which supersedes the treasures of the earth. Your mind will never reside outside of the domain of your treasure. Mathew 6:21 tells us, "For where your treasure is, there your heart will be also" (NKJV)

While Judas sought earthly treasures of thirty pieces of silver, Jesus' heart was set on the things above. As he prayed, he submitted to His Father's will for which He gave his life to fulfil. Judas was bound and focused on the possibilities of the earthly domain, but Jesus kept focus on the spiritual realities. The physical realm cannot supersede the blessings of the spiritual realm. Let us follow Jesus' lead.

ASSIGNMENT
1. Let's do deep introspection. Where is your treasure?

Document your responses to the assignment as well as your challenges and victories.

_____
_____
_____
_____
_____
_____

NO LONGER DENIED

Day 17
Transferred Wealth

Scripture Focus: Matthew 2:1-15

In the year 2006, John operated as a clothing trader and travelled overseas to purchase items for resale. The local currency plummeted in value against the US currency. This induced an internal panic which was easily arrived at as the uncertainty of the future screamed at deafening pitches. To counteract his fears of the future he needed knowledge, knowledge which is embedded in the wealth of the spiritual domain. A wealthy person is one who has learned how to receive in the physical realm what is already known in the spiritual.

After the birth of Jesus and the visitation of the wise men, His life was in danger. According to Mathew 2: 13-14:

NO LONGER DENIED

Now when they had departed, behold, an angel of the Lord appeared to Joseph in a dream, saying, "Arise, take the young Child and His mother, flee to Egypt, and stay there until I bring you word; for Herod will seek the young Child to destroy Him." When he arose, he took the young Child and His mother by night and departed for Egypt..

The wealth of the spiritual domain was transferred to Joseph. This was well needed knowledge, which he acted upon. There was impending danger, but Joseph was unaware. Similarly, there are things that will have adverse effect upon us, but we are unaware of them. The good thing is heaven knows. The word of God tells us in Psalm 139:4, "Even before there is a word on my tongue, behold, O LORD, You know it all." Since God, who is a spirit knows it all, it is in our best interest to connect to that wealth. We need that wealth to be transferred to us.

ASSIGNMENT

1. Be committed to a closer relationship with the all-knowing God, from whom you can receive wealth transference.

Document your responses to the assignment as well as your challenges and victories.

_____

_____

MIND RENEWAL TRANSFORMATION DEVOTIONAL

PART 4:
SEE THINGS DIFFERENTLY

Day 18
DEFILED BY YOUR WORDS

Scripture Focus: 1 Samuel 17: 45-46

The word defile means to damage the purity or appearance of, mar or spoil. Goliath defiled the army of Israel with his words. He belittled them with his utterances. When David came on the scene David did the same to him. He classified Goliath as an uncircumcised Philistine. Goliath cursed him (words) by his gods and David prophesied to him by his God, Jehovah.

We must understand that words are so powerful they can defile or spoil our future. A young lady was married to a young minister. He started receiving dreams and messages of him going to far-reaching countries. He shared them with his wife, and she said, "God did not call her to that, so he is on his own." They got divorced a few years later. He is presently in a different country. She spoke against the future that she did not want to be part of.

David also spoke against Goliath's future when he told him, "This day the LORD will deliver you into my hand, and I will strike you and take your head from you." (1 Samuel 17:46. NKJV). He ended Goliath's future first with his words. The battle between Goliath and David was truly between a dead soldier and an alive shepherd boy. This is an excellent principle for us to apply daily in our lives. Let your words decide the outcome of the battle even before your physical body becomes engaged.

ASSIGNMENT
1. Open your mouth and send your words into battle ahead of your physical presence.
2. Let your words dictate the outcome.

Document your responses to the assignment as well as your challenges and victories.

_____
_____
_____
_____
_____
_____

MIND RENEWAL TRANSFORMATION DEVOTIONAL

Day 19
CHANGE HISTORY

Scripture Focus: 1 Samuel 17:47-49

The army of Israel was defiled by Goliath. He made a mockery of them. For forty days he dared them to challenge him. This can be a hurtful place to be. Having received years of mockery and defiling from procrastination, I know first-hand the humiliation. Procrastination chained my mind, feet, and hands from going forward. Forward stood before me, but I was not allowed to proceed.

I love what David did – he arrived on the scene and did not just identify the problem, Goliath, but faced off against the giant in the name of the LORD. The enemy received a shocker. Everyone else before David ran away from Goliath. David flipped the script. As you face your Goliath, please understand that you are positioned to change the story. Your next decision has the possibility to rewrite destiny.

MIND RENEWAL TRANSFORMATION DEVOTIONAL

You can decide if history continues on the path that was handed down to you. The course of history is within your domain.

David changed a story that was not his to change. The battle at hand was Saul's, which was the generation before David's time. Please understand there are some Goliaths you will have to fight that were passed down through generations. You are positioned to fix what generations before you failed. In correcting the inherited wrong, you secure a better future for the generations that follow you. Please understand, you did not stumble into this position with this mandate. The future depends heavily on you.

ASSIGNMENT
1. Flip the script today. Yes, change the course of history.
2. Do what the enemy does not expect from you.

Document your responses to the assignment as well as your challenges and victories.

_____
_____
_____
_____
_____

NO LONGER DENIED

MIND RENEWAL TRANSFORMATION DEVOTIONAL

Day 20
Challenged Dogmas

Scripture Focus: John 5:1-9

According to Webster's Dictionary, a dogma is a fixed, especially religious belief or set of beliefs that people are expected to accept without any doubts. Dogmas are good as they allow for well-designed structures. They are based on known information. However, available knowledge might not be the complete truth. Don't be bound to the fear of newly learned knowledge, even if it means our dogmas being challenged. Reject the pull to be short-sighted.

The paralytic man of John chapter 5 who was at the pool of Bethesda, was familiar with this dogma – whenever an angel stirred the water, the first to enter it, would be made whole of whatever disease they had. Jesus challenged him to step outside of that dogma and to embrace a new truth. The new truth was this – Jesus can heal him outside of the regiments of the protocols he was accustomed to. He accepted the challenge and was healed. He learned; healing was not restricted to the previous belief system. A greater truth was that his healing was available outside of his dogma.

Like the paralytic man, there are many persons who have remained in incarcerated positions because their dogmas hold them bound. However, it is time you challenge those dogmas against the word of God. If they are not in cohesion with the word of God, then immediate departure from that held belief is necessary.

ASSIGNMENT
1. Make a list of five of your most important dogmas.
2. Compare them against the word of God. What is in cohesion keep, the others change.

Document your responses to the assignment as well as your challenges and victories.

_____
_____
_____
_____
_____
_____
_____
_____

MIND RENEWAL TRANSFORMATION DEVOTIONAL

Day 21
There is no glory in the usual

Scripture Focus: 1 Samuel 17: 37-39

In a conversation with a friend one day, she said, this is tiring. She spoke of the seemingly never-ending fights. She wanted rest. However, I did not share her sentiments. The fights brought me to a place of excitement. As I am afforded the opportunity to further discover the unknown me and more about God. Each new battle comes with new lessons and revelations. Questions like, how will God move in the next battle and what will be my next conquest?

For David, the battle between Goliath and himself saw him discovering that he was not limited to fighting and being victorious over animals. Although he was not drafted into the army, God positioned him, and he won the battle. We learned from David that battles are not won by titles, positions or by the training of men but by God. God revealed himself as the great El Gibor-Mighty Warrior. We learned also, God will allow a crisis to become active, before defeating the enemy. He is a God of timing.

The glory of this victory was infused by it not being won in the usual. Saul gave David his armor, but David took it off. David decided that, this battle will be won but not on the determinants of the physical domain. When it is done outside of man's capabilities, God is glorified at a higher dimension.

ASSIGNMENT
1. Stop fighting in your own strength. Turn the battle over to God.
2. Let Him direct you to your victory.

Document your responses to the assignment as well as your challenges and victories.

_____
_____
_____
_____
_____
_____
_____
_____
_____
_____
_____

NO LONGER DENIED

DAY 22
Benefit of Past victories

Scripture Focus. Numbers 13:1-33

The song writer penned the words, "He will do it again, just take a look at where you are now, and where you have been. Hasn't He always come through for you, He is the same now and then, you may not know how, you may not know when, but He will do it again." This song is one of a deep call to have confidence in the God who gave you the victory in the past, now in the present.

The Israelites were devastated as they listened to the reports of the returned spies who had gone down to Canaan. They said the land is rich, it floweth with milk and honey. But the people are giants and we are like grasshoppers in comparison. The thought of dying at the hands of giants, crushed their spirit. Their confidence in God to give them the victory disappeared. The mistake was, they failed to

NO LONGER DENIED

remember past victories. Which were, the demonstrated power of God through the plaques on Egypt, the parting of the Red Sea and the killing of the army of Egypt that pursued their freedom. Didn't God deliver? Renew your mind with this indelible truth; the victories of the past are given to us to be used in the future as a reminder and encourager, that victory lies just beyond the barriers.

For the Israelites one of their barrier was the Red Sea which was physical. Another was wrong perspective, which was psychological-of the mind. The barrier pushed them to see the opposition as giants and themselves as grasshoppers.

A comparison was done, and the barrier seemed bigger. Their minds rendered them defeated. To enjoy the Milk and the Honey, they must get pass the barrier-the giants.

ASSINGMENT
1. Make a list of the last three victories God gave to you.
2. Write them somewhere that will be visible daily unto you. Let this be a reminder to you of the victory winning God you serve.

Document your responses to the assignment as well as your challenges and victories.

_____
_____

MIND RENEWAL TRANSFORMATION DEVOTIONAL

Day 23
Amplified testimonies

Scripture Focus. Exodus 14:1-31

A barrier is positioned to increase the testimony of the breakthrough already orchestrated.

Red Sea Barrier: The Red Sea served as a barrier between the Israelites and their destiny. This means that anything worth having is worth fighting for. Your destiny awaits you, behind the barrier. A barrier is positioned to increase the testimony of the breakthrough already orchestrated. Barriers promote creativity and determination. They also serve as a compass in redirecting us to dependence on God. As you renew your mind, be conscious, humongous barriers stand between major victories. The old fable says, the hotter the battle, the sweeter the victory. Therefore, rather than getting flustered, get excited when you see a barrier.

MIND RENEWAL TRANSFORMATION DEVOTIONAL

A dear friend of mine was instructed by the Holy Spirit to begin a ministry in a community in Jamaica. She obeyed and got a place to rent. After a few meetings, she was approached by a sorcerer of the said community. He told her, he is god, and this is his territory and she is not needed there. She told him she will stay until God tells her to leave. She became sick and had to be in much prayer. Members began leaving one, by one, until the church was almost empty. God spoke through a young prophet and declared growth. With much fasting and prayer, the change has come. Today the church is growing as God keeps His promise. After the barrier, the blessed testimony.

The magnitude of the barrier is an indication of the size of your testimony. If you allow the size of the barrier to derail you, you will be robbed of a huge testimony.

ASSIGNMENT.
1. Repent of making God small and the barriers big in your mind.
2. Expand your mind to the vastness of who God is. Elevate Him above all your challenges
3. Make notes of your progress.

Document your responses to the assignment as well as your challenges and victories.

NO LONGER DENIED

MIND RENEWAL TRANSFORMATION DEVOTIONAL

Day 24

Seeing beyond closed doors

Scripture Focus. Ruth 1, 2, 3, 4

Until life's journey has come to an abrupt closure, there will forever be doors providing openings and closings. The closed door you're seeing today might just be that push you now need to uncover what has been waiting for you for years. Many persons have been living below their full potential because they failed to recognize the God-given opportunity that a closed door presents.

Simone's relationship broke because of infidelity, poor communication, and financial strains. She was devastated and relieved. She watched persons who were less committed, insensitive, uncaring, and self-centered stayed together, but at thirty-three years old she is single. Again, she has failed was the perpetual thought that refused to

NO LONGER DENIED

divorce her. She stopped exercising, abandoned her strict diet, and became less social. She slipped into depression.

The broken relationship was a heavy and decisive closed door for her.

Like Simone, we can be so stuck in the bitterness of the closed door that we are blinded to the great prospect staring us right in our faces. The victory that awaits you beyond the barriers are too much to not pursue. With the help of family, friends and the church, Simone has begun her healing process. She went back to furthering her education, bought a new vehicle and has new goals and determinations.

In the book of Ruth, Ruth lost her husband and was childless. She was poor and went to glean. She met the owner of the property and they got married. Boaz her new husband impregnated her. He was wealthy and she became joint owner to his business. There is life after every closed door.

ASSIGNMENT
1. Identify the closed door that paralyzed you. Get up and start living again today!

Document your responses to the assignment as well as your challenges and victories.

MIND RENEWAL TRANSFORMATION
DEVOTIONAL

NO LONGER DENIED

MIND RENEWAL TRANSFORMATION
DEVOTIONAL

PART 5:
Vision Instead of Sight

VISION INSTEAD OF SIGHT

Day 25

Perspectives

Scripture Focus: Hebrew 11:1

Some years ago, I was travelling with a friend who was a mechanic by trade. We saw a badly damaged vehicle. I saw a wreck, but he saw opportunity and profit. Both of us saw the same vehicle but from different perspectives. Your attitude and actions are greatly affected and determined by your perspective. That perspective is fueled by the lenses from which you look. Are you seeing through the eyes of God or man, through spiritual vision or physical sight?

Hebrews 11: 1 says, "Now faith is the substance of things hoped for, the evidence of things not seen" (NKJV). Hoped for speaks to spiritual lenses; things seen to physical lenses. Faith is the perspective from which you must receive your dictates or instructions from. Let the eyes of faith be your forever personal navigation system. Faith challenges you to trust that which is not within human comprehension.

Recently, I was told a story of a Christian businessman, who heard in his spirit, to withdraw all his money from a trading company. He obeyed and called his broker with instructions to do withdrawal immediately. Ten minutes later, the broker called back asking, "How did you know?" The Christian businessman replied, "Know what?" The broker said, "The Company just went under." His perspective of the company changed as he received spiritual navigation which he received and accepted by faith. Faith saved him millions and years of sacrifice. Will you allow faith to work for you?

ASSIGNMENT
1. Do a recollection of two incidents where you sacrificed vision for sight. Look closely at what you lost and what you could have gained.
2. Now purpose to develop relation with faith, your navigational system. Let faith be the angle of your perspective. Share with someone your new tour guide.

Document your responses to the assignment as well as your challenges and victories.

VISION INSTEAD OF SIGHT

MIND RENEWAL TRANSFORMATION DEVOTIONAL

Day 26
Visions vs. Sight

Scripture Focus: Ezekiel 37:1-14

A dear friend of mine graduated from a University in Canada with a bachelor's degree. I learned of a vacancy for which she was qualified and informed her. This job would secure her with twice her present salary. But she cited the challenges that came with the job. Challenges she was not equipped to handle. The job she was doing was outside of her training and passion, but it was a low challenging job, a safe zone.

Nelson Mandela said, "There is no passion to be found playing small – in settling for a life that is less than the one you are capable of living." Living a life that is less than your maximum requires no effort and is easily achieved by

VISION INSTEAD OF SIGHT

forsaking vision and focusing on sight. Vision sees beyond sight. Vision roams the streets of the terrains where sight has failed to see. My friend refused to see through the lenses of vision and remained stuck at sight.

According to Ezekiel 37:1, "The hand of the LORD came upon me and brought me out in the Spirit of the LORD, and set me down in the midst of the valley; and it was full of bones." (NKJV) God showed Ezekiel a vision of hopelessness and death. And as the vision continued, He showed him restoration. Sight saw only hopelessness, but the lenses of vision saw restoration. Let us refuse the temptation to reside at sight.

ASSIGNMENT

1. Is it truly over? Is it truly dead? Or is it an awesome opportunity for the power of restoration to be employed? What is it you have given up hope on? Ask the Lord if His desire is burial or restoration. Whatever He says, pursue with all diligence.

Document your responses to the assignment as well as your challenges and victories.

_____
_____
_____
_____
_____

MIND RENEWAL TRANSFORMATION DEVOTIONAL

Day 27
Become a Planner

Scripture Focus: John16: 7-16

Some persons have fallen in love with doing a vision board. This ranges in terms of months and years. It is laced with their goals and the expected time frame for accomplishment. They then strategically decide how they will make this their reality. They understand that the season to ensure what is reaped tomorrow is now.

This takes us back to vision. Hear what the Bible says in Proverbs 29:18a, "Where there is no revelation, the people cast off restraint." While we are living in the now, we must begin to envision the future and begin its creation. This is a tactical futuristic investment. Mr. Barry Watt, former bearer at the Development Bank in Kingston Jamaica, told me a secret. He said he has three major yearly spending: back to school, vehicle insurance and licensing. He went into a partner plan and schedule his withdrawal for July month end (back to school), and the other for the month the vehicle is to be licensed and insured.

Unlike many parents, Mr. Watt is not bombarded with the stress of getting his children out to school, because he planned properly. He secured the future while living in the present. I like when Jesus said it was necessary for him to leave. If he doesn't leave the comforter will not come. He explained to the disciples that His leaving is to ensure a beautiful future for them. Jesus planned their future before He left. The Holy Spirit came and empowered them for ministry.

ASSIGNMENT
1. Create a vision board with a short-term and a long-term goal. The short-term goal must contribute to achieving the long term one.
2. Research and implement strategies to effectively pursue your goals.
3. Get an accountability partner to help you stay the course.

VISION INSTEAD OF SIGHT

Document your responses to the assignment as well as your challenges and victories.

MIND RENEWAL TRANSFORMATION DEVOTIONAL

Day 28
In Spite Of!

Scripture Focus: Mark 16:6-7

In an interview with Roland Martin, founder of Curator News, Culture and Lifestyle, Bishop Jamal Bryant spoke about his infidelity that led to a divorce and the almost total destruction of his ministry. Jamal said, "When I went through a divorce, it wasn't between just me and my ex-wife. It was 12,000 people who were members of my church going through it at the same time, whose hearts were broken, whose expectations were absolutely dashed." He admitted that the problem was not with his ex-wife but with him. He had flaws. Jamal and his ministry were restored and saw new families joining his congregation.

This is similar to what happened with the Apostle Peter. Peter was the cursing and fighting disciple. He denied Jesus and fled the scene. However, after Jesus' resurrection, He said, "Call my disciples and Peter." In other words, Peter, with all your flaws, come. Later Peter preached the first message after Pentecost and in Acts 2: 41 and the results were tremendous. "Those who embraced his message were baptized, and about three thousand were added to the believers that day." Jesus saw beyond sight. He looked ahead in time and refused to leave this mighty preacher behind. Peter had cracks but was a mighty preacher. Your cracks or flaws have not rendered you dead or useless. In spite of your cracks, Jesus have not given up on you.

ASSIGNMENT

1. List two times you allowed your cracks to prevent you from grasping the wealth God had for you. Stop pretending about your cracks.
2. Identify what you could have done differently. At the next available opportunity, do it! Function from your place of vision.

Document your responses to the assignment as well as your challenges and victories.

_____
_____
_____

MIND RENEWAL TRANSFORMATION DEVOTIONAL

Day 29
Vision supersedes Sight

Scripture Focus: John 11: 1-44

Be willing to not be driven by the movement of the crowd but by the direction of your destiny.

Living a life that is less than your maximum requires no effort and is easily achieved by forsaking vision and focusing on sight. Vision sees beyond sight. Vision roams the streets of the terrains where sight has failed to see. The popular current takes us to the average, the norm, what is expected, the easy. But what if your destiny is waiting for you in the abyss of the uncommon or unpopular?

In September 2011, the world was changed by the events of terrorists. Three planes were captured and pursued to the killing of thousands. When the planes hit the Twin Towers in New York, persons were instructed to evacuate but first responders went in. They went where others ran from. They understood the principle: Be willing to not be driven by the movement of the crowd but by the direction of your destiny. In pursuing your destiny and fulfilling your mandate, be purpose driven. To accomplish this, you might need to go against the tide or the current. This requires strength, self-confidence, and focus.

In the account of John 11, we see Jesus went against the tide. He heard that Lazarus was sick but instead of going to heal him, he waited until he was dead. Then he went and raised him from the dead.

Jesus if you love Lazarus, why wait until he is dead? Why has Jesus delayed your healing, breakthrough, or victory? Like Lazarus, it was for the glory of God. Lazarus was resurrected which was a greater demonstration of God's glory, than if he was healed of his sickness.

ASSIGNMENT

1. It is time to do the great exchange. Where have you followed sight and not vision?
2. Make your list! Change that going forward, exchange sight for vision.

Document your responses to the assignment as well as your challenges and victories.

VISION INSTEAD OF SIGHT

MIND RENEWAL TRANSFORMATION
DEVOTIONAL

Day 30

Unique by your Flaws

Scripture Focus: Judges 6:1-23

Your uniqueness is embedded in your flaws and these "flaws" may position you to be used in powerful ways. For example, in the Bible, Moses said, "but I am slow of speech and slow of tongue." (Exodus 4:10 NKJV), Jeremiah said, "Behold, I cannot speak, for I am a youth." (Jeremiah 1:6a NKJV) Gideon said, "Indeed my clan is the weakest in Manasseh, and I am the least in my father's house." (Judges 6:15 NKJV). All three highlighted their weaknesses according to societal standards but God used them mightily.

An unknown author left us a powerful lesson in the popular story of the crushed $20 bill. A professor crushed and stepped on a $20 note, then asked the class who wants it. After persons indicated they wanted it, he explained the lesson. No matter how he treated it, it did not lose its value, hence persons still desired it.

On our journey in life, we will fall many times; we will feel worthless, but no matter what happens, or what may happen, you'll never lose your value in the eyes of God—dirty or clean, neatly dressed or not, you are still priceless. Your value doesn't depend on what you do or who you know; rather, it comes from your own uniqueness. Never forget this."

A young man in deep meditation realized that his enemy was not the system, economy or those who had expressed their hatred for him. He discovered that his primary enemy was himself. He made the wrong choices and was reaping the fruits of his choices. He realized he needed to emancipate himself from himself. He focused on the winkles, dirt and every flaw he had instead of his uniqueness and his value because of the wrong choices he had made., As you renew your mind, always remember your value is not what society says but what God says. You are valuable.

ASSIGNMENT
1. Do you know your value/ worth? Pursue a journey of discovering your true worth.

Document your responses to the assignment as well as your challenges and victories.

MIND RENEWAL TRANSFORMATION DEVOTIONAL

Day 31
Cracks and flaws

Scripture Focus: Jonah 1:2, 4: 9-11

Some years ago, John, a young minister was very condemning. He paraded his righteousness. He looked down on others who were not in his righteousness category. John met a beautiful young lady and they got engaged. Several months before the scheduled wedding date, they had sexual intercourse. He was crushed and cried as he saw himself as the biggest failure. An older pastor learned of his situation and told him, "Now you are equipped to minister to the hurting people."

Because of his own sin, he was now removed from the high seat of condemnation to the place of restoration.

MIND RENEWAL TRANSFORMATION DEVOTIONAL

In the book of Jonah, the people of Nineveh's wickedness had reached the point where it warranted judgment. But God in his mercy extended grace to them by sending the prophet Jonah to preach against them. God presented both options: judgment and restoration. They chose restoration and repented of their sins.

The preacher Jonah was angry at God for forgiving the Ninevites. Although he preached the word and it was received and adhered to, he was disappointed. He wanted the wrath of God to be released but God gave forgiveness.

ASSIGNMENT
1. Remember your own cracks and flaws as you judge another person's shortcomings. Appreciate people's journeys and find one person and help in whatever way you can.

Document your responses to the assignment as well as your challenges and victories.

_____
_____
_____
_____
_____
_____
_____

VISION INSTEAD OF SIGHT

MIND RENEWAL TRANSFORMATION DEVOTIONAL

CONCLUSION

Your 90-day mind renewal journey through the three-part Mind Renewal Transformation Devotional has come to an end. This should never be considered a conclusion to your mind being renewed but rather the completion of a stage or level. The transformation must continue. Romans 12:2a, which states, "And do not be conformed to this world, (mind of the world) but be transformed (to the mind of Christ) by the renewing of your mind" (NKJV), must remain the new dictate being adhere to. Purpose to resist the mind of the world and embrace the Mind of Christ. The pull to backslide to function from the mind of the world will be your constant foe. Be constant in your conviction of never relinquishing the growth and renewal that you have attained. Your mind is at a wealthier dimension and there are more levels to conquer.

As a man thinks, so is he. You are your thoughts. Your thoughts proceed from your mind; therefore, you are your mind. I encourage you to continue your mind renewal

VISION INSTEAD OF SIGHT

journey with my book, Mind Colonization. Let us look closely on the colonization of our minds. Is your mind Colonized? If yes, what territory is responsible and what is the culture and language of that kingdom?

ACKNOWLEDGMENTS

The trilogy Mind Renewal Transformational Devotional series is a by-product of the book Mind Renewal Biblical Secrets To A Better You. The spiritual warfare that ensued during the writing and publishing of the door opener, was super intensive but the Holy Spirit provided a task force to withstand the enemy's onslaught with effective fervent prayers. One of the many prayer sessions lasted thirteen (13) continuous hours. To list the names of the prayer warriors who have been sowing their time and prayers would be too lengthy. I take this opportunity to thank all those who have and continue to intercede on the behalf of my family, myself and our endeavours. Whenever these books are read or shared, your input will be felt.

Special thanks to my first editor and publisher, Cameka Taylor and the Extra Mile Innovators team. Your contribution to this ministry is indelible. You coached me well.

Deep appreciation to my new editor, Juan Lynch. Your humility is breath-taking. I look forward to working with you on many more projects.

VISION INSTEAD OF SIGHT

A big thank you to Hillary Dunkley Campbell. You function as one that is under divine command from heaven to encourage me.

To my Wife Sherene Badjnaut Morrison. God knew I needed your strength and support. He has blessed me with you my GIFT. Thanks for without complaint proofread and first edit all manuscripts. Love you.

ABOUT THE AUTHOR

Jamaican born, Rev. Leostone Peron Morrison, is the author of the book, Mind Renewal: Biblical Secrets to a Better You, from which this devotional series was birthed. He has served as an Assistant Pastor and Guidance Counselor at the Ministry of Education in Jamaica. Currently, he is a Probation Officer in St Kitts and Nevis.

Rev. Morrison is the founder of Restoration of the Breach International Ministry, of which the Restoration of the Breach School hosted on the Thinkific platform is a subsidiary. He is the founder of Next Level Let's Climb Bible Study Ministry. Bathroom cleaning was his first ministry assignment.

He is a graduate of the Jamaica Theological Seminary and holds a bachelor's degree in Theology, with a minor in Guidance and Counseling. He acquired a diploma in Biblical Principles from Victory Bible School, and a certificate from the International Accelerated Missions School. Rev. Morrison is married and has four sons and one daughter.

MIND RENEWAL TRANSFORMATION DEVOTIONAL

NOTE: For feedback, consultation or speaking engagements contact Rev. Morrison at restorativeauthor@gmail.com. Kindly submit a review on Amazon or the platform where you bought this book. Thank you.

VISION INSTEAD OF SIGHT

www.ingramcontent.com/pod-product-compliance
Lightning Source LLC
Chambersburg PA
CBHW071310060426
42444CB00034B/1754